LOST LINES OF ENGLAND
STRATFORD-UPON-AVON TO GLOUCESTER

ROGER NORFOLK

Stratford-upon-Avon
Stratford Racecourse
Milcote
Long Marston
Pebworth Halt
Honeybourne
Weston-Sub-Edge
Willersey Halt
Broadway
Laverton Halt
Toddington
Gretton Halt
Hayles Abbey Halt
Winchcombe
Gotherington
Bishops Cleeve
Cheltenham Racecourse
Cheltenham Spa St James
Cheltenham Spa Malvern Road
Churchdown
Gloucester (Central)

FOREWORD

The railway that connected Stratford-upon-Avon with Cheltenham was a late addition to the GWR's network. It provided the West Midlands at its northern end with a direct route to Gloucester and thence to Bristol and the West Country, or Newport for south Wales. Passenger and freight trains to such destinations quickly populated the route, and the line even became the forefront of GWR innovation when the first streamlined diesel railcars provided an express service between Cardiff and Birmingham in the 1930s.

Without passing through large centres of population, local traffic would not be heavy and single coach trains often sufficed for passenger demand. Local freight traffic consisted of agricultural supplies inwards, with the fertile land producing animal, vegetable and occasionally mineral products in return. Wartime generated more traffic, with RAF airfields constructed around the Honeybourne area and rail-connected stores depots both there and at Long Marston.

However, from the late 1950s, the double-edged sword of increasing road transport and railway rationalisation undermined the line's usefulness. Local trains had been withdrawn by 1969 and through services could be diverted to other routes, so closure became increasingly likely during the early 1970s. The decision came in 1976 with a derailment at Winchcombe and a week later the line was closed. All track was quickly taken up, except for that between Honeybourne and the Long Marston Army camp, with buildings demolished or left to vandals. Delightful views of rural landscapes, fields, farms and pretty villages, the steep, rolling Cotswold Hill scenery to the east and fine views to the Malvern Hills to the west would, it seemed, be lost to railway travellers forever.

Here is the story before closure, from primitive tramway beginnings to its route construction in the early 20th century and concluding with end of steam working in the mid-1960s.

INTRODUCTION

Many quarry and mine owners of the late 18th and early 19th centuries used the advantages of tramway or plateway systems for moving wagons around their sites. One such, Charles Brandon Trye, the owner of quarries at Leckhampton, near Cheltenham, had developed his system during the 1790s, and, with the opening of new docks in Gloucester, now proposed a nine-mile tramroad to take his stone to port. Not only would this benefit his business but a branch into Cheltenham could bring coal and other commodities into this growing and fashionable town. Parliament approved the scheme in 1809, so the Gloucester & Cheltenham Tramroad (G&CT) was built and opened on 4th June 1811. Using a gauge of 3ft 6ins and for commercial services only, it was always horse-worked and even continued to operate after the coming of the main line railways some years later.

Stratford-upon-Avon was also notable for the construction of an early tramway, but this standard gauge line was to be the first part of a far more grandiose scheme. Birmingham, the 'City of a

Thousand Trades', and the heavy industries of the Black Country to its west had been relying on waterways for transport, but the advantages of rail systems were becoming clearer. A proposal was put to Parliament for a 'Central Junction Railway or Tramroad' to provide a rail link from the canal basin at Stratford-upon-Avon to the River Thames to reach London and its docks. Assent for the Stratford & Moreton Railway Company (S&M) to build the first section to Moreton-in-Marsh was granted on 28th May 1821, which also included a branch to Shipston-on-Stour. The line to Moreton was opened on 5th September 1826 and the branch ten years later. As at Gloucester, this was a horse-worked tramway, but here passengers could also be carried. However, no further sections of the original proposal were authorised, so without continuation south from Moreton-in-Marsh, the original ambitions for the tramway were not fulfilled and the line settled to a rural existence.

Whilst these early tramways were important in their own ways, neither would form any part of the eventual rail link between Stratford-upon-Avon and Cheltenham. The G&CT was too circuitous, lightly laid and of narrow gauge to be upgraded but the S&M did fare a little better in that it became connected to the Oxford, Worcester & Wolverhampton Railway (OWW) at Moreton-in-Marsh after that line opened in 1853. In 1859, the part from there to Shipston-on-Stour was converted into a steam-worked branch line and worked as such until closure to passengers in 1929 and freight in 1960. The route north from Shipston-on-Stour to Stratford-upon-Avon was never upgraded and remained a horse-worked tramway until falling out of use in the 1880s, with final abandonment after World War I. In any case, by 1859, Stratford-upon-Avon was already being connected to two main lines, as we shall shortly see.

In the mid-1830s, two proposals were being considered to link Gloucester and Cheltenham into the expanding main line network. One was by the Birmingham & Gloucester Railway (B&G), who wanted to bring products of the West Midlands to Gloucester Docks, whilst the other was to connect Cheltenham to the GWR Paddington to Bristol main line at Swindon. Both proposals had surveyed almost identical routes between Cheltenham and Gloucester

and their Bills were passing through Parliament at the same time, so clauses were inserted to use a common route and for each company to construct half. Thus, assent was granted to both the B&G and Cheltenham & Great Western Union Railway (C&GWU) on the same day, 21st June 1836.

It was agreed that the C&GWU would build the line northwards from Gloucester whilst the B&G build southwards from Cheltenham. However, their track gauges were different, the B&G using standard gauge and the C&GWU GWR broad gauge, so the route between Gloucester and Cheltenham would need to be of mixed gauge. The C&GWU started construction from Swindon but fell into hard times and could only reach Cirencester. The B&G, clearly concerned, decided to complete the C&GWU's half of the route to Gloucester, but, as now the sole operator, laid only standard gauge rails. This opened for traffic on 4th November 1840. Meanwhile, with the C&GWU still in financial trouble, the GWR took over to complete construction into Gloucester and on to Cheltenham. Gloucester was reached in July 1844 by broad-gauge trains to a new station adjacent to that of the B&G, but Cheltenham was not reached until 23rd October 1847 and was achieved by building a loop line that bypassed their Gloucester station and adding broad-gauge rails to the B&G route. The GWR also provided its own terminus at Cheltenham. By this time, the B&G and other companies had merged under the Midland Railway (MR) umbrella, which later became a constituent of the London, Midland & Scottish Railway (LMS).

Each railway operating on a different gauge was a problem for goods in transit, and Gloucester was one location in the south of England at the forefront of this issue. It was not so bad when the two stations in Gloucester were adjacent but this became a bigger issue when direct Cheltenham trains used the new loop line. To provide transfer arrangements, a station was created on the loop line, called T Station, and equipped with turntables and a rail line to transfer carriages between there and Gloucester station. However, this arrangement only lasted until 1851, when a line entered Gloucester from the southwest direction that provided through GWR running to south Wales, thus increasing the importance of this station. The loop line and T Station were dismantled and all Cheltenham trains used Gloucester station, where a reverse for London trains was therefore necessary. By the early 1870s the GWR realised that a change of thinking was needed, and from May

1872 only standard gauge GWR trains operated into Gloucester and Cheltenham.

A footnote may be appropriate as to the fate of the original G&CT tramway. This had been purchased jointly by the B&G and C&GWU in 1836, principally for them to obtain access to Gloucester docks. Whilst not suitable for conversion to main line standards, it was allowed to continue operating, but by 1859 traffic was so poor that closure was the only option and traffic ceased from 1st August of that year.

Meanwhile at Stratford-upon-Avon both the 1852 GWR London to Birmingham route to its north and the 1853 OWW Oxford to Wolverhampton route to its south had left the town high and dry. Both companies were keen to build branch lines into the town and obtained Parliamentary assent for their proposals. The year 1859 saw construction in both directions, southward from Hatton by the Stratford-upon-Avon Railway (SOAR), and northwards from Honeybourne by the OWW. Although slightly longer, the OWW completed their line first, opening on 12th July 1859, with stations at Long Marston and Milcote to a temporary terminus at Sancta Lane in the south of the town. The SOAR completed their line and opened to their terminus in the northwest of the town at

Birmingham Road on 9th October 1860. Again, there was a difference of gauges. The SOAR had been built in mixed gauge for GWR broad-gauge trains, whilst the OWW had built their line in standard gauge only.

Provision had been made in their original Act for the OWW to continue construction through Stratford-upon-Avon to join with the SOAR near their terminus. This was achieved on 24th July 1861, but trains needed to reverse to serve the SOAR terminus. This inconvenience was eased by the opening of a new, joint station on the connecting route at Alcester Road on 1st January 1863, but the Birmingham Road station was retained for goods traffic and, for a few years, the occasional passenger excursion train. Upon opening, only GWR standard gauge trains could access the new station, with some services continuing through to Honeybourne and further.

This was not the end of railway construction into Stratford-upon-Avon, for a railway was authorised in 1864 to approach from the east. This was the East & West Junction Railway (E&WJR), which had permission to construct a line from Towcester, reaching the town on 1st July 1873. However, being low in funds to build a station on their own line, a connection to the OWW branch south of Sancta Lane was used to temporarily access the GWR Alcester Road station, this situation not being resolved until 1875. This E&WJR line was extended to Broom by means of the Evesham, Redditch & Stratford-upon-Avon Junction Railway (ER&SJR) in 1879 and crossed the Honeybourne line by a bridge south of Sancta Lane. In 1908, these independent companies, plus another further east, were amalgamated to become the Stratford-upon-Avon & Midland Junction Railway (S&MJR). Much later, in 1960, a spur was constructed to enable through running of trains from the S&MJR towards Honeybourne, principally for iron ore traffic from Banbury to bypass the busy Leamington and Hatton main line to reach the furnaces of South Wales.

The land between Honeybourne and Cheltenham did not seem to be of strategic importance to these early railway companies. There were schemes to pass through Winchcombe towards Evesham and Ashchurch, and also from Evesham southwards to Gotherington and Cheltenham, but these came to nothing. The initial idea to connect northwards to Stratford-upon-Avon came from an existing railway south of Cheltenham, the Midland & South Western Junction (M&SWJ), that was already operating between Cheltenham, Marlborough, Andover and Southampton. By the late 1890s it had developed plans to build northwards from their line at Andoversford Junction (on the Cheltenham to Kingham route) direct to the Winchcombe area, and then take an alignment along the western edge of the Cotswold Hills to Stratford-upon-Avon. Here, it was to join with another independent railway, the Birmingham, North Warwickshire & Stratford-upon-Avon Railway (BNR) to provide a new route between the West Midlands and the south. At this point, the GWR began to take notice that a competitor was looking to build through what they regarded as 'their territory'. Accordingly, they developed a parallel scheme to connect their existing line at Cheltenham with the Honeybourne to Stratford-upon-Avon branch. Both proposals were seen as viable and had supporters in Parliament, where, in 1898, both Bills were being considered simultaneously. In the event, only the GWR line was given the Royal Assent, on 1st August 1899.

Construction started in November 1902 from a junction with the Stratford-upon-Avon to Honeybourne branch just north of the latter station. The route proceeded south to pass under the former OWW line east of Honeybourne, so through trains would therefore bypass this station. With steam navvies brought to site to assist the army of human navvies, initial work was relatively easy, with gentle curves, long straights and a slowly rising elevation through to Weston-Sub-Edge and Broadway. This first section was complete to open on 1st August 1904. Onwards to Toddington was more challenging, with more earthworks and construction of the 15-arch Stanway (or Toddington) Viaduct to carry the line over low lying ground. Tragedy struck on the morning of Friday 13th November 1903 when arch No 10 collapsed without warning, quickly followed by arches 9, 8 and 7. Four men died, including the driver of a steam crane working above that fell with the first arch. Construction continued and the extension to Toddington opened on 1st December 1904, and two months later to Winchcombe. This completed stage one of the route.

Building beyond Winchcombe was the subject of a separate contract and was only begun in late 1904. It included Greet Tunnel at this northern end as well as threading the route through a populated area of Cheltenham to the south, so work to build this section would be more involved. To present the complete railway project to the public whilst construction proceeded, the GWR brought two of their motor buses from Cornwall to link Winchcombe and Cheltenham stations and, later, these moved south to work from Bishops Cleeve when the railway reached there.

Greet Tunnel's conditions proved challenging, with the solid, packed clay needing gunpowder for removal and requiring an increase in length from the projected 375 yards to a final 693 yards. When completed, the line to Bishops Cleeve opened on 1st June 1906. Work in Cheltenham was not far behind, even though this had included houses demolished, bridges built, bodies re-interred from a cemetery and a 97-yard tunnel at Hunting Butts, so completion to join the railway at Bishops Cleeve was achieved two months later, on 1st August 1906.

The double-track railway from Honeybourne was now complete, but with its junction at Cheltenham being direct into the Gloucester line, services requiring the town's existing station had to make a reversing movement. A curve to allow direct access, and therefore being the third side of a triangle, had been permitted in the original Act but was never built. Work to construct a new station at Malvern Road on the through route was not ready and did not open until 30th March 1908. From this date, the terminus was named Cheltenham Spa St James and the new, through station Cheltenham Spa Malvern Road. Here, a short bay platform to accommodate reversals for railmotors and autotrains was included.

Work now moved north to provide double track between Stratford-upon-Avon and Honeybourne as well as improvements between Birmingham and Stratford-upon-Avon. At Honeybourne, two extra platforms were provided and two new connecting routes built, one to allow trains to run directly between Oxford and Stratford-upon-Avon and the other to allow trains from Honeybourne station to be routed south towards Cheltenham. Long Marston and Milcote both had second platform improvements. North of Stratford-upon-Avon not only was the route from Hatton doubled, with an extra spur from the Birmingham direction added at Hatton to form a triangle, but a complete new double-track line, the North Warwickshire Line, was created to link Tyseley (Birmingham) with Bearley on the Hatton route. With all these works completed, this new GWR main line between Birmingham and Cheltenham, opened on 1st July 1908.

The GWR were quick to use the route for through services between the West Midlands and Penzance, also Swansea. After World War I, and with the developing holiday market, more regular destinations were added such as Weston-super-Mare, Ilfracombe, and Weymouth. From their introduction in 1934, the first GWR streamlined diesel railcars, nicknamed 'Flying Bananas', worked express services between Birmingham and Cardiff. These were single cars with a driving cab at each end and even a buffet counter inside. During the early 1950s, the nationalised British Railways (BR) re-introduced more named trains across its network, which now included *The Cornishman* on this line as the prestige train between Wolverhampton and Penzance. For the domestic holiday market, Saturdays found many extra workings to and from seaside resorts in Devon and Cornwall up to the mid-1960s.

Local trains served all stations and halts along the line but in two sections. Those from Stratford-upon-Avon called at stops to Honeybourne but then continued to Evesham or Worcester. Up from Cheltenham, the 'Coffeepot' locals, a nickname thought to be derived from the early railmotors, worked between St James station and Honeybourne

using the reversing bay at Malvern Road station. Excursion traffic was attracted, with Winchcombe and Cheltenham receiving special trains of day-trippers; others were race specials to the special platforms at Stratford-upon-Avon and Cheltenham racecourses. The latter would be especially busy during the spring Gold Cup meeting, with empty trains being stabled in sidings along the route before returning to collect the punters.

Long-distance freight traffic carried goods between West Midlands' yards, with similar in Bristol and the southwest and with industry in south Wales. Iron ore traffic between Banbury and south Wales has already been mentioned but there were other trains from that direction, including traffic traded with the ex-Great Central line that served the East Midlands and north. One interesting working was between Bordesley (Birmingham) and Swindon, which often conveyed locomotives and other vehicles to Swindon Works for overhaul or even scrapping. World War II brought an increase, not only with through trains but also generated by the Army Engineers' stores depot at Long Marston and others built at Honeybourne, all these locations being rail-connected.

Each station between Stratford-upon-Avon and Cheltenham was provided with goods facilities to enable agricultural supplies and machinery to be imported, with rich produce from Vale of Evesham farms sent away. Some stations had unique exports, such as furniture from Broadway, canned fruit from Toddington and paper products from Winchcombe. In former times sidings might be served by several trains per day, but by the late 1950s this service had been reduced to one train three days a week.

Such was this decline during the 1950s and 1960s that local passenger trains between Honeybourne and Cheltenham were withdrawn as early as 7th March 1960 and stations closed. Goods traffic began to be withdrawn from April 1949 (Gotherington), with most other sidings and yards surviving into the 1960s, the last closure being Toddington in January 1967. North of Honeybourne, the goods yards at Milcote and Long Marston also closed in the early 1960s, but the Birmingham to Evesham passenger service lasted until May 1969. At Cheltenham both Malvern Road and St James stations were closed on 3rd January 1966 and all passenger traffic diverted to the town's Lansdown station on the former LMS route. The future of the line became very questionable and for some years in the early 1970s closure looked inevitable, but that decision never came and it seemed the line could continue in use for through freight and as a diversionary route. However, the freight train derailment at Winchcombe on 25th August 1976 dealt the final blow which led to the line's closing. Within the next three to four years, track was removed from the Stratford-upon-Avon to Long Marston section as well as between Honeybourne and Cheltenham, with many buildings demolished and others left to dereliction. Between Honeybourne and Long Marston track was retained as a three-mile-long siding to serve the rail-connected Army base.

Just before that fateful derailment, the Gloucestershire Warwickshire Railway Society had been formed to try to influence British Rail to keep the line open or, if unsuccessful, to buy to operate it themselves. The sudden closure of the line and its destruction focused minds onto what could be saved, and, eventually, the route between Cheltenham Racecourse and Broadway was purchased. Track has been progressively relaid and buildings rebuilt to produce a successful heritage railway that accurately re-creates the trains and stations prior to closure.

STRATFORD-UPON-AVON

Hall class No 6930 *Aldersey Hall* is arriving at Stratford-upon-Avon station in the afternoon sunlight of 16th August 1958. Steam worked at this time, this is probably the 5.45pm from Birmingham Snow Hill for stations to Honeybourne, Evesham and Worcester. These 4-6-0 general-purpose locomotives, and their smaller-wheeled cousins the Grange class, were equally at home on passenger or freight trains and others appear in these pages heading a variety of work.

To the right, in the middle distance and partially hidden, is the town's ex-GWR locomotive depot. As a sub-shed of Tyseley (Birmingham) it was responsible for providing motive power for the local lines but, latterly, with the closure of the shed at the S&MJR station, ex-LMS types would visit, some from as far afield as Bedford.

Stratford-upon-Avon
Stratford Racecourse
Milcote
Long Marston
Pebworth Halt
Honeybourne
Weston-Sub-Edge
Willersey Halt
Broadway
Laverton Halt
Gretton Halt
Toddington
Hayles Abbey Halt
Gotherington
Winchcombe
Bishops Cleeve
Cheltenham Racecourse
Cheltenham Spa St James
Cheltenham Spa Malvern Road
Churchdown
Gloucester (Central)

Under power through Stratford-upon-Avon station is ex-GWR 2-8-0 No 3834 at the head of a northbound heavy freight train. Originally, all such traffic passed here for onward travel towards Birmingham or Leamington Spa, but, from 1960, ironstone workings between Banbury and south Wales were routed from Fenny Compton onto the former S&MJR line to then link with the Cheltenham route by the newly built spur south of this station.

Whilst local goods traffic was centred on the town's goods depot at the Birmingham Road site of the first terminus, the station sidings at Milcote and Long Marston were served by scheduled workings between Bordesley and Honeybourne.

Right: The prestige passenger service was *The Cornishman*, a daily train between Wolverhampton and Penzance to which Castle class locomotives were rostered. These powerful 4-6-0 locomotives were the first choice for most GWR and BR (Western Region) express passenger trains until replacement by diesels. Here, No 5015 *Kingswear Castle* is in charge as the Down train accelerates from its Stratford-upon-Avon stop over the original S&MJR junction south of the station. *The Cornishman* ran on this route until September 1962, when it transferred to the former LMS route between Birmingham and Cheltenham via the Lickey incline.

Heavy freight loco No 2813 is passing Stratford-upon-Avon SM Junction Signal Box on its way northwards on 9th April 1958. Here was the site of the 1859 OWW Sancta Lane terminus. The tracks curving away above the train's first four wagons are the spur line to the S&MJR, while the bridge over the railway behind the train carries the S&MJR onwards towards Broome. This would carry traffic for two more years, whereupon the new south spur was constructed and the bridge removed. Immediately beyond that bridge were the Stratford-upon-Avon Racecourse platforms, a very stark location devoid of any buildings or facilities and only used on race meeting days.

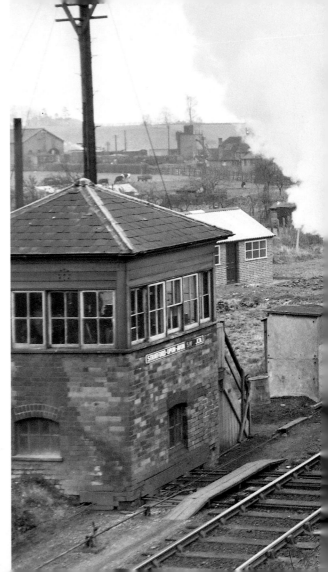

LONG MARSTON

Having passed over the rivers Avon and Stour and through the station at Milcote, the line reached Long Marston. Originally, both Milcote and Long Marston stations were of similar configuration, with a station building, single platform and signal box to the south of a level crossing. Subsequently, each gained second platforms, with those at Milcote changing to the north side of the crossing.

In this scene, the Thames, Avon and Severn railtour of 12th October 1963 is approaching behind ex-GWR 2-6-0 No 6368 and 0-6-0 No 2246. This enthusiasts' tour from London Waterloo reached Woodford Halse via Reading and Banbury, where these locomotives took over to travel by the S&MJR route to Stratford-upon-Avon and then use the 1960 spur for Honeybourne and Worcester.

After other locomotive changes, the train completed its journey at London Paddington that evening.

Stratford-upon-Avon
Stratford Racecourse
Milcote
Long Marston
Pebworth Halt
Honeybourne
Weston-Sub-Edge
Willersey Halt
Broadway
Laverton Halt
Gretton Halt
Toddington
Hayles Abbey Halt
Gotherington
Winchcombe
Bishops Cleeve
Cheltenham Racecourse
Cheltenham Spa St James
Cheltenham Spa Malvern Road
Churchdown
Gloucester (Central)

Opening in 1942, land to the south and east of Long Marston station was transformed into a large storage depot for the Army's Royal Engineers. The external rail connection, internal loop, warehouses, storage sheds and many miles of sidings served the war effort, with an internal fleet of 0-6-0ST locomotives busily employed. With peace declared, work declined, and part of the site was leased during the 1960s to Bird's Commercial Motors to cut up redundant steam locomotives and rolling stock. When the Stratford-upon-Avon to Cheltenham route was closed in 1976, the Army and other railway interests still occupied the site and access was retained by the long siding from Honeybourne.

The Army depot is in the right-hand background as heavy freight locomotive No 3825 heads south with an iron ore train.

The GWR opened a small halt about a mile and a quarter south of Long Marston at Broad Marston in 1904, but with poor patronage and its materials required for the World War I effort, this was closed from 14th July 1916 and dismantled. The local inhabitants had to wait until the 1930s for a replacement, built some 350 yards to the south at Pebworth.

Here, a GWR diesel railcar is approaching its call with, seemingly, no passengers to pick up. This is one of the later builds, with a less streamlined and more angular design, used for local passenger and branch line work. This railcar is probably one of the fleet allocated to Worcester depot for this type of work.

HONEYBOURNE

Honeybourne station was never on the direct route between Stratford-upon-Avon and Cheltenham, but local services from Cheltenham used the West Loop to access its platforms. Here, Pannier tank No 8491 is arriving at Honeybourne station on 17th October 1959 with the single coach, all stations and halts 'Coffeepot' train from Cheltenham Spa St James. The summer timetable for 1959 shows five such trains each way Monday to Friday, and a service of six on Saturdays plus two shorter trips between Cheltenham and Broadway. One service was also extended to and from Moreton-in-Marsh each day. There was no Sunday service. This 1959/60 winter timetable would be the last for these trains since they were withdrawn on 7th March 1960. Note the interesting array of starting signals for the adjacent platform.

Back on the Cheltenham main line and the sight of BR Standard Class 9F No 92224 with an iron ore train approaching Honeybourne West Loop Signal Box and heading towards Broadway. The bridge in the background carries the Oxford to Worcester main line over this route. The signalman has given the driver a run along the main line as opposed to a stop in one of the Down loops.

The working timetable for 1962 shows four day-time iron ore trains regularly diagrammed for this route, but demand for the UK product was waning and on 1st March 1965 the spur at Stratford-upon-Avon was closed after just five years of use.

Pannier Tank No 4614 is working a local freight from Cheltenham past Honeybourne West Loop Signal Box. Here, Up and Down loops were constructed in 1960 as a refuge for iron ore trains to stop for water and, if required, a crew change. Passing behind the box on the extreme left is access to the Down loops. This signalbox was built at the same time as the loops, the original box of this name being sited north of the main line bridge and adjacent to the west loop junction to Honeybourne station.

Ex-GWR 2-6-0 No 4358 is seen here in charge of an Engineers' train at Weston-Sub-Edge in 1958. The Honeybourne to Cheltenham route had a history of poor drainage due to the clay base on which the track was laid. Here, one line has been dug out to remove the clay, with the formation rebuilt ready to take a new top layer of ballasted track. On completion, the line on which the train is standing will be similarly upgraded and this extensive work was required at many sites along the line during the 1950s. Each location took many weekends to complete and single line working was introduced under electric token operation to maintain normal serivces. To break up long block sections, even temporary signal boxes were provided. The current operators are still finding problems with poor sub-soil damaging the formation and thereby requiring attention.

Castle class No 7014 *Caerhays Castle* is passing through the closed station at Weston-Sub-Edge on 31st August 1963 with the 8.02am Wolverhampton to Ilfracombe holiday train. Originally called Bretforton and Weston-Sub-Edge when opened in 1904, the name was shortened three years later to become more in keeping with the station's location. With a goods loop and single siding, local produce was exported on the daily local freight trains. However, both passenger and goods traffic declined after the war, causing the station to be reduced to an unstaffed halt, with its good facilities being withdrawn in September 1950. Station closure occurred with the rest of the line's stations and halts in March 1960.

BROADWAY

A small halt was provided around three and a half miles south to serve the village at Willersey, but the next station down the line was at Broadway. This had been the limit of operations when the first section of new railway was opened in 1904.

This uncluttered view of the station looks north and shows the typical GWR station architecture whose single roof not only covered the station building but also formed the canopy for waiting passengers. This design graced each station on the line between the junctions at Honeybourne and Cheltenham Lansdown.

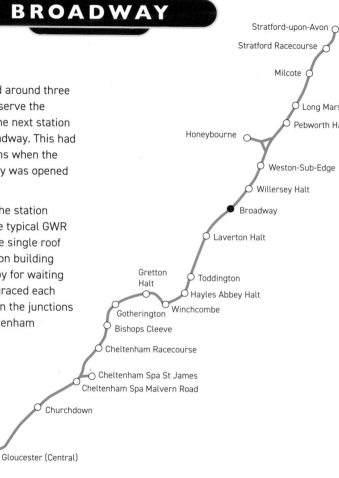

Stratford-upon-Avon
Stratford Racecourse
Milcote
Long Marston
Pebworth Halt
Honeybourne
Weston-Sub-Edge
Willersey Halt
Broadway
Laverton Halt
Gretton Halt
Toddington
Hayles Abbey Halt
Winchcombe
Gotherington
Bishops Cleeve
Cheltenham Racecourse
Cheltenham Spa St James
Cheltenham Spa Malvern Road
Churchdown
Gloucester (Central)

Grange class No 6827 *Llanfrechfa Grange* has charge of a Birmingham Snow Hill to Weston-super-Mare train as it passes through Broadway station on 20th July 1963. The goods yard was on the opposite side of the main Oxford to Worcester Road and was not only busy with products for and from the rural economy but also output from a local furniture factory. Also notable was the popularity of the local hunt and its associated activities – a special horse loading platform was even provided at the north end of the station.

Laverton Halt, between Broadway and Toddington, was opened in August 1905, a year after the line had been opened to Toddington. Here, and at Willersey, the platforms were of wooden construction with pagoda-style waiting shelters provided on each. As with other halts on the line, it was just long enough at 158 ft to take a railmotor or autotrain with a trailer coach. The 2.15pm Saturdays Only from Broadway to Cheltenham is approaching with 4575 class No 5514 at the head, and its three standard coaches will overhang the platform.

TODDINGTON

Besides freight to and from West Midlands yards, through services from further afield also used the route. On 29th August 1962, Modified Hall class No 6984 *Owsden Hall* is making good progress through Toddington station with the 11.45am Crewe to Bristol fitted freight. Other long-distance services seen in 1960s working timetables included Sponden (Derby) and Eastleigh, Boston and Cardiff, Dringhouses (Sheffield) and Cardiff and also Grimsby and Stoke Gifford (Bristol). Not all services used the whole route as some left or joined at Honeybourne as appropriate.

In former years, Toddington was an important location for the examination of through freight trains, which needed to be seen at 45-mile intervals to make sure all was well, particularly checking for overheated axle boxes.

Stratford-upon-Avon
Stratford Racecourse
Milcote
Long Marston
Pebworth Halt
Honeybourne
Weston-Sub-Edge
Willersey Halt
Broadway
Laverton Halt
Gretton Halt
Toddington
Hayles Abbey Halt
Gotherington
Winchcombe
Bishops Cleeve
Cheltenham Racecourse
Cheltenham Spa St James
Cheltenham Spa Malvern Road
Churchdown
Gloucester (Central)

On 31st August 1964, 2-6-2 tank No 5545 has charge of the 8.20am Cheltenham St James to Evesham pick-up goods at Toddington, where it will exchange wagons as required. As well as dealing with similar commodities as other stations on the line, at the western edge of the yard was the Packing Shed. This was a privately owned enterprise where produce could be brought in by rail, transferred off site to be processed and canned and then returned for onward transport.

Whilst the station closed with the cessation of the passenger service in 1960, the goods yard remained open and was the last to close on the line, in January 1967.

Hales Abbey Halt was a later addition to the line, being opened on 24th September 1928. The different design of waiting shelter away from the previous Pagoda style is evident. The stimulus for building the halt was the tourist potential of the nearby Abbey ruins and the opening of a new museum there. With the western edge of the Cotswold Hills visible in the distance, heavy freight tank locomotive No 7214 is working a southbound freight through the halt on 29th September 1955.

WINCHCOMBE

Winchcombe became the new southern terminus of the line on 1st February 1905, and this photograph is believed to have been taken on that day. Some staff are proudly standing alongside the railmotor for the photograph. These trains, as seen here, incorporated a small steam engine within the coach body and worked the first services to and from Honeybourne. When the steam engine was at the rear, the driver operated the train from a driving cab at the opposite end of the coach. Railmotors were later replaced by autotrains, where a separate locomotive was coupled to pull and push the train, with the same principle of the driver driving from the coach in one direction.

Stratford-upon-Avon
Stratford Racecourse
Milcote
Long Marston
Pebworth Halt
Honeybourne
Weston-Sub-Edge
Willersey Halt
Broadway
Laverton Halt
Gretton Halt
Toddington
Hayles Abbey Halt
Gotherington
Winchcombe
Bishops Cleeve
Cheltenham Racecourse
Cheltenham Spa St James
Cheltenham Spa Malvern Road
Churchdown
Gloucester (Central)

No 6868 *Penrhos Grange* has charge of a northbound passenger train through Winchcombe station on 7th September 1959. At this point, the railway is curving to alter its direction between northeast and northwest to circumnavigate an outcrop of hills. The station was built in the village of Greet, around a 20-minute walk to Winchcombe itself. With an interesting local town and Sudeley Castle close by, the station attracted excursion trains as well as freight, with exports from a local paper mill contributing to the railway's traffic.

Just beyond Winchcombe the railway passed through Greet Tunnel, driven through a spur of Prescott Hill. This was the tunnel with difficult clay subsoil that required blasting with gunpowder. There were several fatalities amongst the workforce during its construction.

Here, No 5545 has emerged from the tunnel and is approaching Winchcombe station on 12th November 1964 with the 8.20am Cheltenham St James to Honeybourne local freight. There would be no reason to call at the goods yard here as these facilities had officially been withdrawn ten days earlier, although the Down yard remained in use until February 1965, when this and the signal box closed.

A mile and a half after Winchcombe the railway passed through the village of Gretton, where a halt was provided. Two miles further on was the station of Gotherington, where a goods loop and siding were provided. However, neither passenger nor goods traffic developed as hoped, the station being downgraded to an unstaffed halt from the start of 1941. Early closure was not far away, with goods traffic withdrawn from April 1949 and passenger closure in June 1955. In this view at Gotherington, an autotrain powered in the rear by ex-GWR 0-4-2 tank No 1424 is passing, bound for Honeybourne, on 27th February 1960.

Castle class No 5043 *Earl of Mount Edgcumbe* is seen passing through Bishops Cleeve station on 10th August 1962 with a Swansea to Wolverhampton service. Whilst the buildings were of the same GWR design as others on the line, both here and at Gotherington they were attractively constructed of local stone rather than brick. Fortunately, the locomotive survived in a scrapyard to be privately purchased and restored to main line running condition. However, the buildings fared worse and were razed to the ground after closure in 1960, with no trace now remaining.

Castle class No 4096 *Highclere Castle* has arrived at Cheltenham Racecourse station with special train 1X01 from London Paddington on 13th April 1960. This headcode normally denotes a royal train carrying the monarch, but the locomotive is without the required four headlamps and the Queen was not in attendance. Special trains arrived here on race days from all over the south and the Midlands but, without stabling sidings, those arriving northwards continued to sidings and loops further up the line, whilst those arriving southbound continued into Cheltenham. Locomotives were turned at Honeybourne or Cheltenham, as appropriate. The station closed after the Gold Cup meeting in March 1968 but re-opened for the meeting three years later until seeing its last traffic in March 1976. It was not used again after the line closed later that year.

CHELTENHAM

This is the junction at Cheltenham Spa Malvern Road East, where Castle class No 4087 *Cardigan Castle* is taking the Stratford-upon-Avon route with the 1.27pm Newquay to Wolverhampton on 10th August 1962. The lines disappearing in the lower left corner led to St James station. To make way for the Stratford-upon-Avon route in 1906, the original Cheltenham locomotive shed sited in this area was demolished and replaced by a larger shed in the yard at Malvern Road. Also, the original signal box controlling the throat of St James station was replaced by the Malvern Road East box, seen here in the centre distance.

Stratford-upon-Avon
Stratford Racecourse
Milcote
Long Marston
Pebworth Halt
Honeybourne
Weston-Sub-Edge
Willersey Halt
Broadway
Laverton Halt
Gretton Halt
Toddington
Hayles Abbey Halt
Winchcombe
Gotherington
Bishops Cleeve
Cheltenham Racecourse
Cheltenham Spa St James
Cheltenham Spa Malvern Road
Churchdown
Gloucester (Central)

The Cornishman has arrived at Cheltenham Spa Malvern Road station on its way south behind an unrecorded Castle class locomotive. With the main service running to Penzance, at peak holiday times, and especially summer Saturdays, the train would be run in several portions, each serving specific resorts.

Southern Region U class locomotive No 31619 has arrived at Cheltenham Spa Malvern Road station on 2nd May 1959, its last stop before terminating at St James station. This is the 7.50am from Andover, which will work back at 1.52pm for Southampton Terminus. These trains came north via the ex-M&SWJ route to Andoversford Junction and in pre-grouping days used running powers over the GWR from there to reach Cheltenham.

Ex-GWR 2-6-0 No 6326 is arriving at Cheltenham Spa St James on 10th August 1962 with a special excursion from Llanelly. Cheltenham, as a popular tourist town and gateway to the Cotswold Hills, often generated such traffic, but St James station also saw direct scheduled trains to Swindon and London Paddington, Bristol and Cardiff, as well as local trains to Gloucester, Honeybourne and Kingham.

Other facilities here were the town's goods yard and a locomotive turntable that also served the shed at Malvern Road.

One year later and Hall class No 6943 *Farnley Hall* is leaving with the 11.00am excursion train to Weston-super-Mare.

Pre-war, the town's name had become synonymous with high-speed rail travel when the GWR accelerated its afternoon train to London Paddington to become 'the fastest train in the world'.

The *Cheltenham Spa Express* became known as the Cheltenham Flyer, as the schedule of 65 minutes for the 77.3 miles between Swindon and London required an average speed of 71.4 mph. The fastest, on 6th June 1932, produced a record run in 56 mins 47 seconds at an average speed of 81.58 mph by Castle class locomotive No 5006 *Tregenna Castle*.

This is Cheltenham Spa Lansdown Junction, where the GWR route from Stratford-upon-Avon (tracks on the lower left) joined the LMS route from Birmingham (the lower right) to form shared rails to Gloucester. On 25th August 1962, 0-6-0 No 2249 is threading the 4.00pm from Hereford across the Junction onto the GWR route and will terminate at Cheltenham Spa St James. There is another pair of tracks curving away to the left above the first carriage of the train. This was the GWR line to Kingham. From Andoversford Junction on this route, the former M&SWJ line diverged southwards.

Four tracks took the railway from Lansdown Junction through the intermediate station at Churchdown towards Gloucester. This section had originally been of double track but was rebuilt into four during the first years of World War II. Churchdown station dated from February 1874, although two earlier ones had existed, a previous temporary one here in 1842 and a shorter-lived replacement at Badgworth in 1843. Enlarging the line in 1942 required the two platforms at Churchdown be rebuilt into islands, and here, an unidentified 5101 class tank locomotive with a local train is occupying the Up Main. The station's closure came in November 1964, and the four-track section was reduced back to double in 1967.

GLOUCESTER

An autotrain headed by No 1453 is crossing Tramway Junction level crossing at Gloucester on 3rd October 1964. Here, the former companies' combined route from Lansdown Junction separated for each to access their own Gloucester stations. In addition, a sharp curve took trains from the ex-GWR station to their direct London route and on each side of the crossing were freight yards and sidings. The building on the extreme left is the end of the former GWR Horton Road engine shed. The name Tramway Crossing refers to the original G&CT of 1811, which diagonally crossed these tracks at this location.

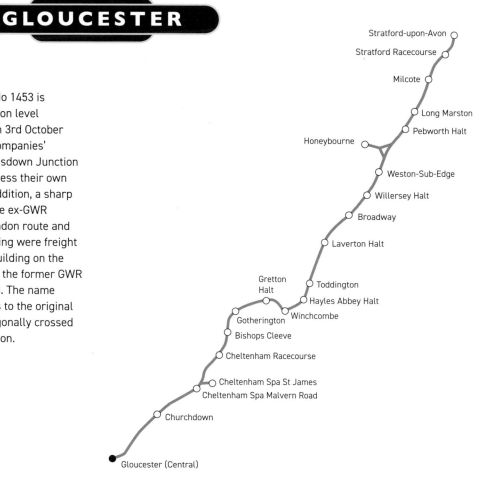

Stratford-upon-Avon
Stratford Racecourse
Milcote
Long Marston
Pebworth Halt
Honeybourne
Weston-Sub-Edge
Willersey Halt
Broadway
Laverton Halt
Gretton Halt
Toddington
Hayles Abbey Halt
Gotherington
Winchcombe
Bishops Cleeve
Cheltenham Racecourse
Cheltenham Spa St James
Cheltenham Spa Malvern Road
Churchdown
Gloucester (Central)

Pannier tank No 9430 heads the Cheltenham portion of a London express out of Gloucester Central station for the last few miles to Cheltenham Spa St James on 3rd October 1964. By this time, London expresses had arrived behind diesel locomotives, with the Cheltenham coaches conveyed to their destination in the manner shown. At Tramway Junction the two routes separated. The further tracks, on which the train is running, serve the ex-GWR station and are signalled with lower quadrant signals, whilst the nearer tracks serve the ex-LMS station with upper quadrant signals.

Ex-GWR 2-6-0 No 7328 is at rest in Gloucester Central station's main platform on 4th July 1959. Two stations served the city for many years, the 1914 GWR station for trains to London Paddington and Cheltenham Spa St James and the 1896 MR station for trains on the Birmingham to Bristol route. Almost adjacent, each was connected to the other by a 190-yard-long footbridge. In 1951, to avoid confusion, BR named the former Gloucester Central and the latter Gloucester Eastgate. However, Eastgate was closed in December 1975, leaving just this former GWR station to serve the city.

CREDITS

Lost Lines of England – Stratford-upon-Avon to Gloucester. Published in Great Britain in 2022 by Graffeg Limited.

Written by Roger Norfolk copyright © 2022. Designed and produced by Graffeg Limited copyright © 2022.

Graffeg Limited, 24 Stradey Park Business Centre, Mwrwg Road, Llangennech, Llanelli, Carmarthenshire, SA14 8YP, Wales, UK. Tel 01554 824000. www.graffeg.com.

Roger Norfolk is hereby identified as the author of this work in accordance with section 77 of the Copyright, Designs and Patents Act 1988.

A CIP Catalogue record for this book is available from the British Library.

ISBN 9781802582024

1 2 3 4 5 6 7 8 9

Printed in China TT200522

Photo credits

© Transport Library: page 13.
© GW Trust (Didcot): pages 14, 21, 27, 30-31, 50, 51, 56-57.
© Transport Treasury: pages 15, 17, 20, 37, 40.
© Restoration & Archiving Trust: pages 19, 24, 29, 32, 35, 36, 39, 43-45, 46-47, 49, 52-55.
© Steam @ Swindon: pages 23, 28, 33, 62-63.
© Roger Norfolk: pages 59, 60-61.

The photographs used in this book have come from a variety of sources. Wherever possible contributors have been identified although some images may have been used without credit or acknowledgement and if this is the case apologies are offered and full credit will be given in any future edition.

Cover: Stratford-upon-Avon.
Back cover: Cheltenham Spa, Honeybourne, Cheltenham.